Don't Let
The
Messenger
They Shoot
Be You!

Bob,
I thoroughly Enjoyed
working with you! Thanks
for all your support. Enjoy
with my best wishes.

A Survival Guide
For Public Speaking

C. Mike Jour

DON'T

MESSEN

THEY

BE

A SURVIVAL GUIDE

LET THE GER SHOOT YOU!

FOR PUBLIC SPEAKING

C. Mike Jousan

Clear Communication Books
Scottsdale, Arizona   1992

DON'T LET THE MESSENGER THEY SHOOT BE YOU!
A Survival Guide For Public Speaking

By C. Mike Jousan

Published by:

CLEAR COMMUNICATION BOOKS
6453 North 77th Place, Suite 7
Scottsdale, Arizona 85250

Copyright © 1992 by C. Mike Jousan
First Edition
Second Printing 1999

Library of Congress Catalog Card Number: 91-78373
ISBN 1-881012-07-7: $9.95 Soft cover

Manufactured in the United States of America

www.clearcommunication.com

This book is dedicated to all of you who are uncomfortable, scared, or terrified when you are asked to speak in public. May you find enough encouragement to stand up and take that first step toward the front of the room.

Thanks to the person who gave me the three most important rules of public speaking: Stand up, so they can see you; speak up, so they can hear you; and shut up, so they will invite you back!

Special thanks to my wife and business partner, Vicky, who has never stopped believing in me . . . For believing that this book should be written, for believing that I could write it, and for using her qualities of tenacity, organization, thoroughness, encouragement, and patience to make her belief a reality.

ABOUT THE AUTHOR
C. Mike Jousan

Is an internationally recognized speaker who is one of our nation's experts on communication.

Educated in his native Texas, with graduate study in advanced communications, he received an honorary doctoral degree in 1976.

Mike ran for U.S. Congress in 1978 and served as consultant to the Ford Foundation. In his varied career, he has worked as a college fund raiser, an economic development consultant, a salesperson, a political adviser, a political candidate, and a corporate education trainer.

In 1988, he founded Clear Communication Company, a consulting firm specializing in all forms of person to person communication. He is a member of the International Association of Business Communicators, the National Speaker's Association, and the Scottsdale Chamber of Commerce. In addition to *Don't Let The Messenger They Shoot Be You! A Survival Guide For Public Speaking,* he is the author of *Trash Those Junk Words! Make Your Point Clearly.*

In consulting with corporations, he helps clients become more effective by projecting a positive visual and vocal image. He coaches executives, sports celebrities, and political candidates in on-camera comfort and confidence in high pressure circumstances. He projects a wonderful blend of intelligence, confidence, sensitivity, and humor in his speeches and training sessions.

CONTENTS

CONTENTS

INTRODUCTION

In ancient times, messengers did not live to a ripe old age. While disease and illness sent some to the grave, the most tragic of all the early deaths came when messengers were shot because people did not like the message!

It still happens in the 1990's! **We shoot the messenger!** As you read these words, someone, somewhere is making a speech or a business presentation. Audiences usually listen attentively at the outset, wanting some new and fresh information ... But as the speaker drones on, or gets into a losing battle with audio visual equipment, overheads, or slides, they load their guns (*figuratively*). Thank goodness we are civilized. I know of no **RECORDED** instances of speakers literally being shot, and falling dead behind the podium. You and I both know situations where people go to sleep, start side conversations, lapse into near-comatose states, and make a decision **NOT** to buy a product, approve a budget, try an idea, or whatever it is the speaker wants us to do. We **SHOOT THE MESSENGER!**

Communication is never easy, but this book will decrease your chances of being shot!

I DON'T NEED TO READ THIS BOOK!

You may be saying to yourself. "Public speaking is for the pros and for those who are constantly making presentations to large groups. I never make speeches. I never appear on TV, and I will never need to learn how to do things like that." • • •

THINK ABOUT THIS:

- Every time you verbally communicate a thought or idea to another person . . . you are using a public speaking skill.

- When you are negotiating with another for a certain result (*a large contract or a window seat on the plane*), you are using a public speaking skill.

- When you are urging someone to try your product or service, you are using a public speaking skill.

- Even when you ask or answer a question in a meeting or when walking down the hall, you are using a public speaking skill.

Of course the setting is different. There is something different and special about standing up and speaking to an audience that is sitting down, **WAITING FOR YOU TO SPEAK!** The skills used in front of a large group are the same ones used in a one-on-one conversation or a phone call. You simply adjust the volume, energy, and gestures so that they are appropriate for the audience.

Remember the good news - Public speaking is a **LEARNED** skill - anyone can learn it, and everyone can do it better.

You can learn to use eye contact, rid yourself of **JUNK WORDS**, open and close your message with firmness, and use positive body language to support what you say. Using these skills will bring you confidence and results in every situation.

Whether you are with a major corporation or a small company . . . If you are a top executive or if you were recently hired and are starting your career . . . you should develop your public speaking skills. You will become more confident, comfortable, and convincing in every communication situation.

YOU NEED TO READ THIS BOOK!

NOTICE

This book is in alphabetical order. From **A**drenalin to **Z**ipper, find the information or the "tip" to help you speak better. Jump in and have fun!

DON'T LET
THE
MESSENGER
THEY SHOOT
BE YOU!

A SURVIVAL GUIDE
FOR PUBLIC SPEAKING

ADRENALIN

Adrenalin produces **"extra"** energy that can be measured in your pulse rate, breathing patterns, and sweat glands. You have heard stories about the effects of adrenalin. Imagine you are driving home one night on a lonely road. You come to an accident and discover a person trapped under a car crying out in pain. No one else is around, and you have no lift equipment. You respond to the cries for help, reach under the bumper, and - almost magically - lift the car!

There are many recorded instances of human beings being able to lift many times their weight, all because of adrenalin being pumped into the body. The amazing part of these stories is that the feat usually cannot be repeated once accomplished.

When the adrenalin stops pumping, the body goes back to "normal," and we can lift about as much as we usually can.

Think of your own experience when you are challenged. You can run faster or hit the golf ball farther. Then we should not be surprised when these same things happen at the beginning of a speech! Remember the famous television newsroom scene in the movie, *Broadcast News*? He could not stop sweating!

The person in front of the room whose voice is shaky, whose hands are trembling, and whose tongue is getting tangled up in simple words is a normal person who is suffering an adrenalin attack!

If untreated, such a person might throw up, faint, black out, or turn red! (*The internal mechanisms of the body are likely very embarrassed when they see what we do with their attempt to help us out of an uncomfortable situation!*)

If the adrenalin is allowed to function in an unfocused, negative way, we can have a public speaking disaster. You probably have seen them, and maybe you have had one. Such a bad experience can cause persons to stop speaking **FOREVER**. Their careers and lives can be affected drastically. Such persons need special counseling and professional support. Fortunately, this happens to only a small percentage of people.

Most persons learn to make adjustments and "**control**" the adrenalin. They stand in a rigid position, lock their hands in some fixed position or attach them to a lectern, rock back on their heels, read from a text, and speak in a low monotone as if near death. *(And you thought that was just your boss or your minister!)* Such a person will avoid the dramatic disaster but will bore us to the point of sleep.

There is a better way! First recognize that the adrenalin attack is normal and happens to **everybody**. Do not try to **"control"** it or stuff it back inside yourself. **Let it go . . .** allow it to happen in a positive, focused way. The adrenalin or **"extra energy"** is redirected out to the audience through the hands, the eyes, the voice, and the total body. Edwin Newman says that *we never get rid of the butterflies, and we shouldn't try. We can learn to make them stop banging into each other and fly in formation.*

Begin this process by changing the name of what is happening to you. Stop talking about stage fright, nervousness, fear, or terror . . . start calling it **POSITIVE ANTICIPATION.**

Recall a recent wonderful experience that you knew in advance was going to be wonderful. Did you approach that experience with nervousness, fear, or terror? Of course not! You did the opposite. The experience lay before you and you raced toward it thinking, **"I can't wait,"** or **"Let me at it!"**

This can happen to you - the public speaker - as you walk to the front of the room. When used positively and focused outward, adrenalin can be your friend.

BE THE B.E.S.T.
YOU

Be the B.E.S.T.

Your goal as a speaker should be far more than mere survival of the ordeal! You can get better; you can even be the best! Don't let that scare you! You do not require major surgery. Stay away from those who would put you through a **meat grinder** to clone you as the perfect communicator. (*That's for penguins!*)

While you probably aren't using your talents to full capacity, you already have everything you need to be a very good communicator. Bring them out, dust them off and use them!

Remember the **B.E.S.T.** acronym to be the **BEST** that you can be!

Be Prepared *(See page 30)*

Excite Yourself *(See page 45)*

Shorten *(See page 101)*

Test Run *(See page 109)*

BE PREPARED

This motto has been good for the Boy Scouts for years. Apply it to your presentation process. Preparation is a necessity for a good speech or presentation. Preparation is like that part of the iceberg below the surface that holds up the visible part. It's like the foundation of a building.

It usually starts with an analysis of the audience. Arriving to speak without knowing a lot about the audience is akin to treason! Know their business, their goals, their markets, and their history. Know the people in the room. Be sure that you are answering their questions and solving their problems. Be sure you know what to emphasize and what to avoid!

Develop one major purpose for your presentation. *e.g.* "To sell this company 1,000 units of my product in the next quarter," "To enhance the environmental image of my industry," "To invite investors to invest in XYZ." This purpose must be very clear to you, and everything you say should relate to it.

Organize and tighten your words. Develop a clear and forceful opening and close.

Develop your key points, and stick to them! *(Three is a good number.)* Finish one before you start the next one, and connect them with good transitions.

Body Language

55% OF THE MESSAGE IS BODY LANGUAGE

What you do speaks so loudly that I can't hear what you say! This is certainly the truth whether we are speaking of past performance, reputation, or in the arena of a presentation or speech.

Have you listened to a speech when part of you said the ideas were great, but another part of you could not pinpoint an uneasy feeling about the message? Perhaps you dismissed this as another in a series of mediocre encounters. There is a much deeper reason, mostly subliminal, for these feelings. We as the audience are continually making judgements about the validity of the messages we hear.

When there is an inconsistency between the speaker's words and his or her actions, our brain gets confused, and we will believe the actions first.

What you do with your eyes, hand gestures, body movement, and posture will have a dramatic impact on the meaning of your message.

When your eyes dart about, look up or down, or are not focused, we will perceive that you are not genuine. Your posture and gestures will reveal what you feel about the words you say.

55% of your message is body language. This does not mean that what you say does not count. What this means is that what you say **MUST** be backed up with proper body language for your message to get through.

BREAK A LEG!

When one actor says to another, **"Break a leg,"** that is of course not to be taken literally (*unless you are the understudy and want that part very badly!*). It means, **"Do well"** or **"Do the job that you know you can and we know you can."** You should never approach the podium with doubt or uncertainty. Allow yourself only positive thoughts. You know what you are doing, you have prepared well, and nobody but you can say what you are about to say.

Remind yourself of three things. (you can even keep a list in your briefcase.) **What's good about me personally?** Warm personality? Good voice? Friendly? Good smile?

What's good about me professionally? Good product knowledge? Known for follow-up and attention to detail? Helped develop the product I am selling? Invented it? Twenty years experience?

Why can I do this better than anyone else today? Intimate knowledge of the customer? Totally believe in the product?

Now go and **"Break A Leg!"**

BUT

When you must criticize, avoid using the word **"BUT."**
Most persons will not remember what you said before
the **"but"** - only what you said after. Try replacing
"but" with **"and."**

(Example) "Your performance with the XYZ account
has been wonderful, **but** you haven't touched their other
divisions . . ."

(Suggestion) "Your performance with the XYZ account
has been wonderful, **and** you should now translate that
success into their other divisions . . ."

(Example) "Your speech today was dynamic, **but** . . ."

(Suggestion) "Your speech today was dynamic, **and** it
would be even better if . . .

CHOOSING UP SIDES

They are always choosing up sides! One of the toughest jobs in life is choosing a team when you do not know the capabilities of the people standing in line. Remember the softball game at the picnic? (*Were you the one always chosen last?*)

Every time we encounter people - at a party, in a meeting - we do a quick **"once-over."** In a matter of seconds, we put together a complex picture of other persons - before they speak, show us their business card, or hand us their resumé.

This happens when we stand up to speak. In a few seconds the audience **"pre-judges"** us and decides if they will **tune in** or **tune out**.

Pay attention to the way you enter a room, how you stand at the podium, and the first words you say. **Be certain that the audience chooses you!**

Cliché

A cliché is defined in the American Heritage Dictionary as: *A trite or overused expression or idea.*

When does an expression become a cliché?
Some will say that an expression becomes a cliché when the reverse meaning is true. When you hear someone say, **"To make a long story short,"** you know that you are in for a long, probably boring ordeal!

Clichés are like stale bread. They may keep you alive in a pinch, but no one will rush back for a second helping. Clichés do not make the audience shout **encore**! Remove them from your speech. Find something fresh and exciting to say instead. Be known for your **DIFFERENT** approach. Become quotable.

COMMUNICATION PROBLEM?

Studies indicate that the average worker spends approximately 50% of his/her day communicating. Salespersons, support staff personnel, and top level management may be involved in communication for 75% or more of their work day. Also it is estimated that seventy percent of mistakes in the workplace can be attributed to ineffective communication.

A survey of 400 subscribers to *"Communication Briefings"* revealed what they consider to be the three top traits they desire in employees:

- **Interpersonal communication skills.**

- **The ability to write well.**

- **Good speaking abilities.**

Only 40% of those surveyed placed educational background and work experience in the top three categories.

Roger Flax, President of Motivational Systems wrote recently in the *Chicago Tribune*:

"Companies are finally saying, It's costing us billions of dollars a year in productivity losses because employees don't know how to write or stand up and give speeches."

Lack of effective communication is far more than an irritant; it costs productivity, time, and money. The good news is that communication skills can be **taught** and **learned!** Take action! You can change communication from a problem to a profitable asset that drives your business.

CONVERSATIONAL TEST

••• Apply the Conversational Test

If you want to avoid stilted writing, apply the Conversational Test developed by John Louis DiGaetini of *Hofstra University*. **HOW:** Ask yourself if you would ever **SAY** to your reader what you are writing. For example, would you say, "Enclosed please find the price lists you requested?" You probably would say, "Here are the price lists you requested."

The Conversational Test helps you get rid of business jargon and impersonal writing. It forces you to write in human terms and adds color and interest to your writing.

The same is true when you make a speech, a presentation, or speak before the TV camera. Speak in down-to-earth, easier-to-under-stand words and phrases. Professional interviewers say they want their guests to be concise and direct. When we sit in an audience, we want the same. We will not believe you if you put on airs or use pompous words or phrases.

Use familiar words. Leave in-house jargon, acronyms, and abbreviations where they belong: in-house.

Use active instead of passive verbs. "The order will be delivered next Monday," is not as direct as, "We will deliver the order next Monday."

Get to the point quickly. Put yourself in the seat of the listener, and remember your attention pattern. It's like a curve: we read or listen carefully at the beginning, then trail off. Only something exciting, abrupt, or dramatic will bring us back to attention. So, make your opening fresh, clear, and inviting.

CAUTION:

Do not assume that the Conversational Test allows you to use slang. You still have to assume a proper business tone. Use accepted words and connect them with proper grammar and punctuation.

Remember: If you wouldn't say it in a conversation, don't write it or present it that way.

DEAD AIR

Dead air is OK!

Have you ever heard a speech that sounds as if it were prepared for a radio broadcast? Run-on sentences. No pauses. No time to digest the contents.

It is perfectly acceptable (*and preferred*) for you to pause, reflect, and gain composure. Your audience will appreciate the silence, and you will appear to be thoughtful and under control.

EXCITE YOURSELF

If you want the audience to be excited, then **YOU** must be the most excited person in the room! Your energy, enthusiasm, and excitement will set the tone for the audience's response *(or lack of it)*. Of course your excitement level must be related the product, the audience, and your personal style and comfort level. If you are a Chief Financial Officer delivering a budget to the Board of Directors, you should not act like a carnival barker!

We joke about the salesperson who *loses the sale by showing up!* You are not incidental; you are the central character. You are directly connected to the product, the service, or the message that you bring. Your commitment, enthusiasm, and energy *(or lack of it)* will make the difference in whether the audience tunes in or turns off.

Study your product or service. Know it better than anyone else. Remember what it has done for others. Think of what it will do for your audience today. Then be direct and personal. Share your feelings in an upbeat and positive way. **Excite yourself and we will be excited.**

EYE CONTACT

"REACH OUT AND TOUCH SOMEONE"

We know that we cannot physically touch someone through the phone, but AT&T knew we would understand. A key element in communicating is making a connection. We often express that in physical terms. **"He didn't get through to us in that presentation." "I was touched by her words."** When we communicate one-on-one or in small groups, we usually shake hands. In large groups that is not practical. The best we can do is to touch them with our eyes.

In any presentation or speech, be sure they can see your eyes, and be sure you look at them. Your plan should be to carry on a series of individual conversations. If you do that, everyone will feel involved and will say, **"She talked to me."** Do not scan the room like a windshield wiper. Do not establish a repetitive pattern (*they will feel like ducks in a shooting gallery!*). In a natural fashion, speak individually to everyone.

The benefits? You get immediate **FEEDBACK.** Long before they fall asleep, you will know that their interest is lagging, their stomachs are growling, or that you are not speaking to their concerns or issues. Feedback gives you **CONTROL.** You can shift gears, emphasize or de-emphasize, or stop talking! All because of what you see in their eyes. You also will have more control over your words and phrases if your eyes are focused. Eye contact is the major cure for **"JUNK WORDS"**. **"UHS"** and **"YOU KNOWS"** cannot live long in the speech of someone with good eye contact!

The biggest benefit is **TRUST**. Eye contact is like taking a lie detector test without being hooked up! Unlike in a courtroom, the results of eye contact - good or bad - are admissible in interviews, the handling of tough questions, and the giving of information in the speech or presentation.

If you want to **"MOVE"** them, **TOUCH THEM WITH YOUR EYES.**

FEEDBACK

The Scottish poet Robert Burns asked the Almighty for the power to **"See ourselves as others see us."** He did not get that wish, and neither will we. But we still wish we had that power - to be able to stand back and watch ourselves as we go through life. We would love to be able to see our performance in our business, to observe ourselves in personal relationships, or to watch our golf swing or tennis stroke. Since we cannot do this, we rely on others to watch us and give us their feedback or critique.

Don't let critique scare you. While it does come from the same root word as criticism or critic, its basic meaning is **"to judge."** To grow as a presenter you need honest judgement about your progress.

This is true when you first begin speaking in public and will be true throughout your career, no matter how advanced you are. Bad habits creep in. The same stories are used too often. We become too fond of the sound of our own voice and forget how to stop talking after a reasonable amount of time. Top professionals in every field continue to get feedback; it assures that they remain at the top!

Speakers have been coached and directed since the ancient Greeks practiced oratory. Your task is easier - with **VIDEOTAPE**. Have yourself videotaped in rehearsal and - if possible- when you make the actual speech or presentation. Watch and listen to the tape and learn from what you see. Is your eye contact focused and steady? Is your voice interesting? Is there variety in your delivery? Does the message make sense? Does the person on the tape keep **YOU** awake?

Be open and objective about feedback. A colleague of mine is convinced that the higher we go up the ladder of success, the more difficult it becomes to get and accept honest feedback from those who work for us. I agree. Remember the story of the *Emperor's New Clothes*? The poor fellow was walking around naked, and his loyal subjects were afraid to tell him the truth!

To keep that from happening to you, find someone or hire someone to give you honest feedback. Let them hear and critique your rehearsals, ask you the tough questions, and do a debriefing with you when the speech is over.

Fig Leaf

Reverse Fig Leaf

Weather man

Open

FIG LEAF

A major problem when speaking is determining what to do with our hands. Remember the Bible story of Adam. When he made public speeches, he likely clasped his hands together in front of his body - a position we call the **Fig Leaf.**

Have some fun as you watch speakers. You will see the **Reverse Fig Leaf** and the **Weatherman**. Some speakers hold their hands together as if in prayer; others appear ready to dive into a pool. Others grip their hands together as if wringing out a towel. Others carefully place their fingers together in what appears to be a spider resting on a mirror. *(When the hands move, we have a spider on a mirror doing push-ups!)*

What we do with our hands can be funny or at the least distracting. Hands help us best when we gesture appropriately from an **Open** body position. We cannot use them to gesture when they are held together, stuck in our pockets, or attached to the lectern.

FIRST IMPRESSION

Psychologists tell us that we decide to read a letter or document in the first five seconds after we touch it. We do about the same with persons who stand up to speak! You never have a second chance to make a good first impression. Pay careful attention to your facial expressions, your posture, your dress, and the first words you speak.

(see **CHOOSING UP SIDES**)

Focus person

A focus person is someone in the center of the back of the room. That person is the one who gets your **GRABBER** at the beginning of the speech or presentation. This gives everyone in the room the opportunity to focus on you better for those opening words. This also ensures that everyone can hear you.

Delivering the grabber to the focus person is also good for you. It settles you, focuses your thinking, and establishes a good eye contact pattern. The remainder of the presentation becomes a series of brief one-on-one focused conversations with as many individuals as you possibly can. Find that same focus person (*or someone nearby in the back*) as the individual who will get your closing words.

GOALS

"Wherever you are going,
you will get there faster
when you communicate better!"

C. Mike Jousan

GOALS

No matter what your goals in life are, you will reach them faster if you communicate better. I hear this everywhere in some fashion. A friend of mine says he got only two pieces of business advice from his father: **One, watch your expenses**, and **Two, learn to stand up and talk to people!**

From Iacocca of Chrysler to Carlzon of SAS, the importance of stand-up communication is stressed by business leaders. From your first job interview to your speech before the shareholders when you become the President, you will be judged by the way you present yourself. **Good communicators rise above the rest of the pack!**

If it is not there already, place **BETTER PRESENTATION SKILLS** on the top of your goal list. Come to one of my seminars, take a course, join Toastmasters, and volunteer to speak whenever and wherever you can. All of your other goals will be reached faster when you communicate better.

[AND REMEMBER THIS]

Every presentation or speech should have a goal. Ask yourself, **"Where am I going with this?"** Or better, **"Where do I want the audience to go?"** This is your overall sense of direction - the big picture. As you funnel down (*focus*) from your goal, you will be able to write a title and develop a **"Grabber,"** - those important opening words.

You can then test your key points - do they point toward and support your goal? Does everything I say **"flow"** in the direction of my goal? Do my final words, my close, tell the audience exactly what I want them to do or where I want them to go? If the answers to these questions are clear to you, the message will be clearer to us.

GRABBER

You Can Double Your Income
In The Next Six Months
If You
Follow My Plan!

Does that get your attention? Of course! We often hear something more like this:

"I'd like to take a few minutes of your time today to share with you my plan which is designed to increase your income significantly if you follow it."

The thought is there, but its strength is obscured by extra words that do nothing more than add fluff!

A Grabber is one or two sentences which are carefully prepared, edited, and delivered with power. It's like the headline of a newspaper article or the lead sentence in a paragraph. Its purpose is to grab our attention.

First impressions are always important, and they are critical in the presentation. Your audience will make major judgements about you in the first few seconds. **Grab** their attention at the beginning. Study your goal. In that goal you will find the words for your grabber. Commit them to memory, so that they can be delivered with confidence and power.

Of course you can say, "Good morning!" (*You must be pleasant.*) But then pause, focus on a pair of eyes in the back of the room, and deliver your **GRABBER.**

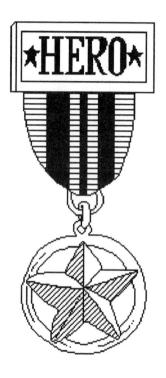

Hero

Who is your **"hero"** or **"heroine"** in the field of personal communication? Ronald Reagan? Jane Pauley? Lee Iacocca? John F. Kennedy? Martin Luther King? Ann Richards? We can learn from others and even **"borrow"** things which work well for them. But we should never try to sound like, act like, or be like *ANY OTHER* communicator. You will be the best communicator you can be when you discover and share with the audience -

"The Best

YOU"

IMPORTANCE

(Can you afford not to?)

The presentation we make is a lot like the clothing we wear. Wearing the appropriate clothing will not guarantee that we will make the best impression or make the sale. It **WILL** guarantee that the impression or the sale will not be negatively affected by the way we dress. When the classic excuse about clothing is given - I can't afford to buy that suit or dress - the response is usually, you can't afford **NOT TO!**

Can you afford not to make the best presentation every time you present? You can't afford **NOT TO!** We all remember the sale we made, the client we have, the promotion we got - all because of a presentation we made. There were other factors, of course, but the initial impression or the final decision usually came down to one specific set of words delivered at one specific time and place!

Cities around the world bid for the right to host the Olympics. Years of research, documentation, and planning - at great expense - go into this process. The final stage in the lengthy selection process for the finalist cities is an appearance before the committee for a **ONE-HOUR** presentation. All the other factors count, but minds are changed in that final presentation.

People judge us by the way we present. If you are a senior executive, your company and your industry will be judged by your presentation. Salespersons can get a foot in the door and win a major client with a strong opening presentation. Politicians win nominations and elections based on their speaking skills - sometimes on one key speech with the right audience. Younger persons begin to advance when someone hears them speak and notices their presentation skills.

For all of us, we never know who might be watching and listening when we present. Planning, preparation, and rehearsal does take time and money. Find the time, and spend the money. **You can't afford NOT TO!**

JOKES

Humor is always a good way to relate to the audience. (*I have heard humor used appropriately in a eulogy at a funeral!*) Humor puts us at ease, breaks down the barriers between you and the audience, and keeps us awake! A joke is one way to use humor, but beware! (See **X-Rated**)

I have three rules for joke-telling. One, be sure that you can tell a joke well. Two, be sure that it is funny. And three, be sure that it has some relation to what you are saying. A presentation is not your audition for the comedy club!

A joke at the beginning has particular hazards. If it falls flat, you begin in a deficit position trying to crawl out of a hole. You are better off starting with a carefully thought-out, well-delivered Grabber.

(See **GRABBER**)

JUNK WORDS

"WELL, I THINK, UH, YOU KNOW..."

Well Uh, fourscore and seven, uh, years ago, you know, I think, our forefathers, uh . . . Uh, ask not, you know, what your country, uh, can do for you . . . Lincoln and Kennedy have every right to be turning over in their graves!

The use of **Junk Words** diminishes your power and credibility. An otherwise good presentation by an intelligent person can sound juvenile when littered with **"uhs," "you knows,"** and qualifiers like **"I think."** Having to search for the message under the junk words is like digging for hidden treasure - we know it's there somewhere, but we lose patience and give up.

A presentation should always move in one direction, from start to finish, like a train on a track. If you backtrack or zig-zag, you lose momentum, and the audience may go off on another track. Junk words take us off thetrack. They make you sound lost even though you may know where you are going.

Junk words are costly! Imagine sending a telegram around the world at an expensive rate per word. Would you throw in some **"Uhs"** for effect? When you speak to others, every junk word you throw in costs you a bit of your credibility and stature.

How do you get rid of junk words? First, count them. This may be painful, and you may not realize they occur when you speak. Videotape or record yourself, or get someone to listen.

Figure out when they occur. When you break eye contact with the audience? When you are trying to figure out the exact word to say next? When you lose your place in your text or notes? When you lose focus?

Pause and think before you speak. The audience will appreciate the **"dead air"** as a time to process what you just said. You will have time to focus your eyes and your thoughts and say something crisply, clearly, and without **JUNK!**

JUST

Remove the word **"just"** from your presentation. In many instances, using the word weakens your presentation and makes you appear unsure of yourself.

Examples:

"I'm **JUST** here today to talk to you about . . . "

"I **JUST** want to show you a couple of examples . . ."

"I **JUST** want you to see the big picture . . ."

NOW . . . eliminate the word **"just"** and see how much more confident you sound.

KEEP THEM AWAKE

If you see the audience starting to look sleepy, don't take it personally! The very best audiences need to be kept awake. We are all products of the television age. Attention spans are getting shorter all the time. We are accustomed to fast-paced, interesting, highly visual presentations of information.

Put yourself in the place of your audience, and make your presentation user-friendly. Speak to their interests and concerns: solve their problems. Involve them with personal examples, group exercises, and question and answer segments.

Avoid anything monotonous in your presentation style - a monotone voice, a repetitive gesture, a cliché, an old story. Mix your visuals, and vary your pace.
Be upbeat, positive, and enthusiastic with your body language as well as your words. Maintain eye contact with the audience. If you start to lose them, do something to get them back.

Be careful of the words you say! Don't say "I want to talk to you today for a **few** minutes about a **few** things". . . They won't believe you! Keep your promises. If you say, "my presentation today will last fifteen minutes," stop talking at thirteen or fourteen; they'll be counting! If you say **"In closing," CLOSE!**

Every presentation should be lively and interesting, but watch yourself at those crucial times: after lunch, after dinner, before the break, or just before the cocktail hour. Always keep the room as lighted as possible. A darkened room may make your visuals look sharper, but when the lights are turned up, your audience may be stretched out on the floor!

(See **SHORTEN, EXCITE YOURSELF**, and **SIMPLIFY**.)

LISTEN

An old proverb states that since we have two ears and one mouth we should listen twice as much as we talk! The reverse is more likely true. There are many excellent reasons for listening more than we talk, and learning and practicing better listening skills. Specifically related to presenting and speech-making, you should:

LISTEN BEFORE YOU ARRIVE

One of the best ways to analyze an audience is to ask questions and listen to the answers. Listen to the person who invited you and others who will be present. If you are seeking business from a company, listen to the marketplace, the competition, the financials . . . The ideal presentation is a series of answers to the questions of the audience.

LISTEN WHILE YOU PRESENT

Don't wait for Q & A at the end of the presentation. Listen to the mood of the room, to others who have spoken, to the way you are introduced.

During the presentation get feedback by listening with your eyes as well as your ears. Are you getting positive vibrations? Are they with you? Can they take more? Should you stop talking?

When formal Q & A begins, follow these rules: Establish eye contact and listen very carefully to the questions. When the person has **finished** the question (not before), pause briefly, and then deliver your answer.

LISTEN AS YOU LEAVE

Keep your ears open during the final handshake and pleasant goodbyes. You will often get signals about next steps to take, who to contact . . . and it's not bad to listen to people tell you that they liked what you had to say.

You must use words to present, but remember the power and control you gain by pausing, remaining silent, and **LISTENING.**

MILITARY RULE

When in doubt use the Military Rule of communication!

- **Tell them what you're going to tell them.**

- **Tell them.**

- **Then tell them what you told them.**

NATURAL & REAL

"Present like you talk to us!"

Sometimes when I give that advice, I see a look of disbelief which says, "You haven't heard **me** talk!" This is what I mean.

Some people stand up to make presentations, and they use a stilted voice. Their sentences are long, drawn-out, and complicated. Their gestures are awkward and stiff. They do not sound or look **REAL.** Of course you must elevate your volume and expand your energy to match the size of the audience, but . . .

When you present, use the same style, word choice, descriptions as you do when you are talking. Sound like yourself! Caution: not the kind of talk you use at the water cooler discussing the weekend. Not the way you talk when you describe your golf game or when you have just missed a short putt! Talk the way you talk when you are talking at your best.

Present the way you talk in an important meeting with important people in the room. Present the way you would talk in a job interview.

DO:

• Present in simple, easy-to-understand language. That means short words and short sentences. (*Even sentence fragments are fine.*)

• Be concrete and specific, not abstract and general.

• Use familiar stories and examples.

If you are natural and real, we will understand you, believe you, and remember what you say.

NERVOUSNESS

What? Me Speak? Now?

The business equivalent of the "Last Mile" or walking the "Gang Plank" is the walk to the podium to make a speech or presentation. We would do almost **ANYTHING** rather than speak in front of an audience. *The Book of Lists* gives a fascinating perspective. **Of the Ten Worst Human Fears**, our **NUMBER ONE FEAR** is speaking before a group. Death is number seven!

Tony Hulman owned the Indianapolis Speedway. He gave the opening introduction to the Indianapolis 500 on Memorial Day for many, many years. Only those in the announcer's booth knew that he used a prepared text printed on cue cards to help him deliver his message. The astonishing part of the story is that he always said only **FOUR** words! "Gentlemen, start your engines." (*The first year with a female driver he <u>did</u> say, "Lady and gentlemen, start your engines."*)

Hulman's example may be extreme, but we all must deal with the uncomfortable feeling caused by a fear of public speaking. We call it nervousness, stage fright, apprehension, discomfort - even terror!

This fear strikes everyone, and it's a **REAL** fear! While you face more **actual** physical danger playing with a snake or walking unprotected in a very high place, when you walk to the front of a room to speak, your body is also processing **FEAR**. (See **ADRENALIN** for more information.)

OH! NO! (How to avoid problems)

- **Trust no one** to follow instructions!
  Even at the best facilities, there is
  always *something that needs to be*
  changed.

- **Arrive early** and check the room.

- **Is audio/visual** equipment working properly?

- **Bring your** own microphone. . .
  Make sure you have extra batteries?

- **Are your slides right side up**? In the proper order?

- **Do you have** drinking water at the podium?

- **Is the lighting** in the room satisfactory?

- **Have a second copy** of your speech
  notes in a separate place!

PRACTICE, PRACTICE, PRACTICE . . .

**"Someone, somewhere out there is practicing . . .
and if I am not practicing, when I come up against
him, he will win!"**

Those words were spoken by U.S. Senator Bill Bradley
when he was still a New York Knick, but they apply as
well to his speeches as a politician.

Athletes, musicians, and actors achieve greatness
through preparation. After watching Ben Hogan play a
masterful round of golf, someone asked him about his
"lucky" shots. Hogan replied, **"The more I practice,
the luckier I get!"**

Presentations which appear spontaneous and effortless
are the finished products after hours of practice.
Excellent answers to tough questions are the result of
rehearsals designed to polish those answers. The most
successful speakers practice; so should you! Record
yourself, play the tape, and during the playback ask
yourself . . .

How do I sound? Are my sentences short and my words understandable? Do my stories and illustrations support my message? Are my verbs in the active voice? Do my opening words grab attention, and does my close tell the audience what to do - clearly? Is my tone of voice upbeat and positive? Is there enough variety in my volume and pace?

How do I look? Am I using good eye contact? Do I need to read my text or use as many notes? Is my posture commanding? Am I dressed properly for the occasion? Am I believable? Do my visuals support my message? Am I talking to them rather than the audience?

How often should you rehearse? Every time you speak! You will feel more comfortable, and your audience will see the difference in your confidence, organization, and style.

PRESENT WITH A PURPOSE

A presentation should have a clear beginning, a strong ending, and should tell us what to do and where to go! Rarely do we stand up just to **GIVE INFORMATION**. We want the audience to **DO** something. We want them to buy our product, act on our ideas, vote for us in the election, or hire us to handle a special project. If your purpose is very clear to you, then it will likely be clear to us.

Remember that each of us is bombarded with and must process vast amounts of information every day. We are always making choices - to listen or not listen, to buy **A,** or **B**. When you look out at us, you cannot expect automatic attention and uncluttered, receptive minds. You are competing for our attention, our support, our money.

Front-load the message. Tell us at the beginning what you want us to do, where you are leading us. State your **PURPOSE** clearly. Your first impression is not just how you look and how you sound - it's also what you say.

Choose your opening words carefully, and deliver them firmly.

Then, support your purpose with stories, visuals, data, and examples that are understood by and clearly relate to the audience. Ask two questions of everything you plan to say: does it further my purpose? and does it relate clearly to the audience?

Make your ending strong. We usually remember the last thing you say. State your purpose again clearly and tell us specifically what you want us to do. The three military rules of communication still apply: tell them what you're going to tell them, tell them, and then tell them what you told them.

The sermon and the graduation address should make us feel good. **Your presentation should move us to act!**

I have a question!

I have a question!

Over Here . . . I have a question!

QUESTIONS & ANSWERS (Q & A)

The impact of a good or **very good** presentation can be diminished by poor handling of questions and answers. Here are some tips:

REHEARSE YOUR ANSWERS

When Henry Kissinger was Secretary of State, he approached the podium one day, opened his notes, and asked, **"Does anyone have any questions for my answers?"**

The reporters laughed, but that's the way to do it! Think through the toughest questions you might get, plan the answers, and rehearse them. Make your answers crisp and tight, and don't **OVERANSWER**!

REMEMBER THAT IT'S STILL YOUR SHOW

Do not give up control when your formal presentation stops. You have an agenda: stick to it.

TREAT QUESTIONERS WITH CARE

Don't play favorites or put people down. The same is true with questions. Do not let your answers, your tone of voice or your body language convey the message "What a stupid question."

MAINTAIN CONTROL OF THE ROOM

Share your answers with persons other than the one who asked the question. Always bridge back to your agenda no matter what the question might be. Set limits on time, numbers of questions, and any other ground rules before you begin. When you finish, do not simply say thank you. Deliver a mini-close - state your objective one more time.

QUOTE

Don't end your speech with a quote!

You have a golden opportunity to restate your objectives at the end of your speech. Don't be tempted to use a quote. Using someone else's words weakens yours. You want the audience to remember **YOUR** words and ideas.

(see **PRESENT WITH A PURPOSE**)

Reading a Speech

A young Scottish minister preached his first sermon in a new church. In the Church of Scotland, there is a person called a beadle who is assigned to help the minister through the service. After the service the minister asked the beadle for his feedback on the sermon. His reply . . .

"I have three comments: In the first place you read it, in the second place you didn't read it well, and in the third place, if you had read it well, it wouldn't have been worth hearing!"

Don't read speeches or presentations! Children appreciate bedtime stories: adults do not! You cannot keep eye contact when reading. Your energy level is never as high when reading, and your voice volume is muffled.

If you **must** read something, be sure you read it **well**.

Sometimes there is a compelling reason for something to be read: a quotation that must be exact, language that must meet some legal requirements, etc. Be sure that you practice reading the passage several times, so that your eyes do not remain "glued" to the page. Use the technique of finishing the last part of each sentence or thought in a pair of eyes in the audience - not back in the words. **When you reach a period or comma, you should be looking at a person!**

(To be sure that the words are worth hearing, see **BE PREPARED**)

SHORTEN

When we talk about great speeches, Lincoln's Gettysburg Address is always mentioned. While Lincoln's ideas that day were inspiring, we remember that his speech contained simple down-to-earth language (*Written on the back of an envelope*) and was **brief**. The speech was so short that there are no photographs of Lincoln making the speech. He was on his way back to his seat when the photographer got his first picture.

Audiences in those days could sit through a speech or sermon which lasted for hours. Not only could their posteriors tolerate sitting that long, but their minds could process and remember far more information than we can today. We are more accustomed to short sound bites and brief stories. Our attention spans are dramatically shorter!

One rule of public speaking should **ALWAYS** be followed: Stop talking before they expect or want you to stop!

SIMPLIFY

Use your simplest language when you present. When I was growing up in a small town in Texas, my English teacher, Miss Harris, asked me one day, "Do you want to get out of this little town?" When I eagerly replied, **"YES!"** She advised calmly, **"Learn a lot of words."**

I soon learned what she meant. The places we go in life - geographically, financially, socially, - are largely dependent on our vocabulary. The richer our vocabulary, the richer we will be. Our thoughts and actions will be more creative, more precise, and more convincing. I believe this deeply, and I urge you to believe it. Study words and increase your vocabulary. It will set you apart.

HOWEVER, when you come to the front of the room, keep your big words in your brain, and translate them to their simplest possible form. Our attention spans are very brief. We must process an incredible amount of information each waking moment. Even if we are willing, we are no longer able to sit through and comprehend complicated material and big words.

Our brains are overloaded and nearly **saturated**. Major publications like the *Wall Street Journal* have lowered the grade level of their information content. Are their readers slower or not as smart as they once were? Of course not - they are busier.

We live in the Information Age. More is available, we need and want more, but we want it faster and simpler. A rule for business writing is, "Don't send them to the dictionary or the thesaurus." Apply that same rule when you speak.

Keep it simple! Let them hear how deep your thoughts are - not how long your words are. JFK's speechwriter may have been thinking, "It is no longer appropriate for a citizen to ascertain the level of benefit which she or he might wish to accumulate from his geographic governmental unit . . . " when he had the President say, *"Ask not what your country can do for you."*

STYLE OR SUBSTANCE?

Many persons are shocked when they discover that the non-verbal part of the communication process is so important. The accepted analysis is:

WORDS	7%
TONE	**38%**
BODY LANGUAGE	**55%**
TOTAL	**100%**

When we stand up to communicate, **93%** of our impact is non-verbal.

Should we go to acting school? To have fun or to become an actor, yes, but probably not to help us in the business world. Think of the ways that style concerns us. We pay careful attention to the image of our product or service. We spend large sums of money on **"packaging."**

We **"Dress For Success,"** and we **"manage"** the impressions others have of us when they enter our showroom or visit our office.

We also must be concerned about our speaking **"Style."** Some honest, intelligent politicians do not get elected because their speeches and TV appearances are dull. Some authors write compelling books but do not do well when they are interviewed. We joke about keeping our engineers and technical people **"locked-up"** because they cannot **"sell"** things that they invent or make. The result is that more time, energy, and training budgets are being spent on the improvement of speaking style.

Do not neglect substance! Without substance, style is empty and hollow. Snake-oil salesmen could never stay long in any town. Ad campaigns will fizzle if our products break. Behind every **"sizzle"** there better be a steak! You need well-written speeches and presentations just like you need good products and services. Then use style to get our attention. Style opens the door. Style invites us to hear your substance. Good words will tell us a story, but good words **SUPPORTED** by non-verbals (*tone and body*) will convince us that you believe those words and we should too!

TELEPHONE

PRESENTATIONS

They can see you through the phone! The way you sound paints a clear picture of the way you look. Your tone of voice tells us how you feel, what you believe, if you are prepared and organized. It also tells us if we have your attention, if others are in the room, or if you are trying to do two things at once. **Suggestions:**

- **Sit up straight**, or better yet - stand.

- **Keep your eyes** focused.

- **Keep one hand free** to gesture; your voice will sound more energetic and upbeat.

- **Prepare a written** agenda. Follow it.

- **Front-load** your important information. Be pleasant, but state your purpose early in case they have to hang up.

- **Don't let someone** catch you off guard. If you are not ready when they call, offer to call them back. Then prepare for the call.

CAUTION Technology is wonderful, but it can depersonalize. Use the speaker phone **only** for cost-saving conference calls, and use the car phone **only** for personal calls or emergencies.

TEST RUN

Call it rehearsal, practice, or a test run - just do it! The speaking process is never complete without a test run. Record what you say, and if possible, videotape it.

The mirror is not good enough for a test run: the feedback is too gentle from your own face! Another person can help if they promise to be honest and you promise to listen!

Can you rehearse too much? I usually hear this question from those who refuse to make the commitment to rehearse at all. (*I suppose it is POSSIBLE to rehearse it to death.*) If you need a rule, rehearse it once for the content, and then rehearse it at least twice for the non-verbal factors (*tone of voice, junk words, posture, gestures, and eye contact.*).

Remember that the person who stands before us looking so natural and at ease with the material and the audience likely gets that way from planned and proper rehearsal.

U – WILL THEY UNDERSTAND?

The next time you speak or write, ask yourself, **"Will people understand what I am trying to say?"**
Remember, 25 million North Americans read below the fifth grade level, and 35 to 40 million read between the fifth and eighth grade levels.

Even if the listener or reader is many levels higher, the problem of understanding remains. Your readers and listeners suffer from an information **"overload."**
Thousands of messages bombard us every day. Advertisers reach us in fifteen second commercials; major news stories are given to us in a few seconds on the evening news; and *USA TODAY* appeals to us with simple language, brief stories, and striking visuals.

Be known as one who "gets to the point," talks in down-to-earth language. and is easy to understand.

- Choose the shorter, more familiar word instead of the lengthy, more complicated one.

Get to the point quickly and **"front-load"** the message! We form impressions in a matter of seconds. If that impression is blurry, confusing, or complicated we may leave you - never to return.

* Use visuals that illustrate what you say. Remember the old proverb which says, "A picture is worth a thousand words."

  Limit the words on your visual. A slide or overhead should have concise, key words that support what you are saying.

In a world characterized by an information **"Glut"** or **"Overload,"** the simple message will get through, get our attention, and be remembered.

Very unique?

Can something be **VERY** unique? Maybe when
someone can become **VERY** pregnant
. . . or **VERY** dead.

The American Heritage Dictionary defines **UNIQUE**
as: **1.** Being the **ONLY** one of its kind; sole. **2.** Being
without an equal or equivalent; unparalleled.

It is impossible for anything to be **VERY** or **TRULY**
unique. Using the word in this manner weakens your
point and causes you to lose your audience!

Take this challenge:

Never qualify words such as unique, perfect, round,
complete, pregnant, or dead . . .
They stand **ALONE.**

VISUALS

Talk in bumper stickers or T-Shirts!

In countless meeting rooms around the world, people are standing up in front of a room, pointing at a flip-chart, slide image, or overhead. That image is tiny, complicated, difficult to read, and almost impossible to understand. That person is more than likely using the cliché, *"As you can see on the chart . . ."*

I was walking through an airport and saw a message on a T-Shirt. The message got my attention, but it was complicated and lengthy. I nearly got arrested, because I found it necessary to follow the person past several gates, peering over shoulders, running into people, until I finally got the complete message. No matter what your medium is, keep the message down to a few key words, about as many as you would put on a T-Shirt or bumper sticker!

Visualization

The golfer **"sees"** the perfect shot fly over the water and land softly on the green. When the chef gathers fresh ingredients from the market, he pictures the perfect meal on the table. Salespersons picture a completed sale, and the artist visualizes the result when the first brush touches the canvass.

Will such visualization help when you stand up to speak in front of a group?

ABSOLUTELY!

We **always** "visualize" the future - usually negatively. We **expect** the traffic to be bad. We **know** we will not find a parking place. We hit an **old ball** when we come to the water holes. We expect that they will nod off and not laugh at our jokes . . . before we approach the podium!

The evidence suggests that our **"picture"** of the future has a significant effect on what that future will be like. We do not always get everything we want, but we usually get what we **expect**. A positive expectation draws us toward a goal or result like a magnet. Visualization can play a major role in the making of a presentation or speech.

Visualization is not a substitute for the work of presentation-making. You must know your subject, you must prepare, and you must rehearse. But in addition, get a clear picture in your mind of your desired result. **"Hear"** the applause of the audience. **"See"** the smiles on their faces. **"Enjoy"** the fact that they have bought your product, service, or ideas.

Believe in yourself and the anticipated success of your presentation. Walk up to the platform with a **"NEW BALL!"**

WHATEVER HAPPENED TO ENDING A SENTENCE???

You can get from here to downtown on a bus or whatever . . .

A pig, a pony, a train? What is this statement telling us?

"Whatever" as an ending? We hear this all too often . . . On television, from interviews with ordinary persons on the street to highly educated professionals, this ending is loosely used.

Whatever is an appropriate word to use when we are bridging from one idea to another. It is not to be used as an ending or a filler. Whenever you listen to a thought or idea, you will unconsciously loose the impact if the speaker ends with "whatever."

Make a conscious effort to avoid ending with "whatever." If you must use the word, continue the thought and end the sentence.

Words, Tone, Body

It's not that words are unimportant; they are **limited**.
(See **STYLE OR SUBSTANCE?**) A word is a
mechanical device which we use to label a person, an
object, or a thought. The meaning is not found in the
word, but in the mind of the person hearing the word.
Our tone and body language can dramatically change
the perceived meaning of a word.

Dull speakers can make exciting speeches sound dull.
*(Or the opposite - we say that we could be inspired
listening to some persons read the phone book!)* Words
are only words, and if we speak them without emphasis
and feeling, they are only worth about **7%** of the
communication process. The good news is that we can
change that number!

The other **93%** of the message - tone and body - are
what **we** bring to the mix! **We** bring interest and
excitement by the way we say the words. **We** inspire
confidence and commitment by the way we look and
the way we stand.

Tone is the way we speak - the sound of our voice. Be sure that you are breathing properly, so your voice sounds full and rich. Emphasize words with the variety of your voice. Vary the pace of your delivery. Be certain that you can be heard by everyone in the room.

Body is everything physical that we can see. Use gestures that are natural and support the words that you are saying. Stand up or sit up straight. Smile as much as you can (*appropriate with what you are saying*). Use eye contact to make a clear connection with the audience.

When you approach the front of the room, all you can bring with you are your words, tone, and body. The very best communication takes place when all three work together in harmony. If we hear you say something, and your tone of voice and body language support what you are saying, we will understand you, believe you, and follow you!

X - RATED

BEWARE! Avoid saying anything that anyone might consider to be profane, vulgar, or in bad taste. An innocent "hell" or "damn" might be terribly offensive to someone in the audience. The use of such a word might cost you a sale or a promotion. There are enough colorful words available; you need not be **"off-color."**

The same advice applies to words, language, or jokes that are racist, sexist, or a put-down to someone in the room. I once heard a presentation in which a reference was made to Pearl Harbor. The person making the presentation did not know that a key person in the audience had a Japanese spouse and was extremely sensitive to that issue.

Pay attention to special concerns and taboos in certain regions, companies, or nations. The safest path is to make sure your presentation is rated **G!**

YOUR MOMENT OF TRUTH

In the language of customer service, every contact the customer has with any representative of a company is a **"Moment of Truth."** For those who present, our presentation or speech is our **"Moment of Truth."** People judge our competence, our reliability, our product, our company - even our entire industry - based on how we present. Our presentation or speech is the first connection of what we are selling with the customer.

Even if you do not have a product in your hand selling in the traditional sense, you are always selling. Very few of us are as fortunate as the television commercial character who sells Hondas. The point of the Honda commercial is that his product is **SO** outstanding that even the worst salesperson cannot ruin a sale! This is usually **NOT** the case. The audience can be turned off as well as turned on by the way we present.

In the political world, Mario Cuomo is still spoken of in relation to one moving speech at the Democratic Convention. Chrysler received loan guarantees from Congress based on the speaking skills of Lee Iacocca. In conference rooms all over the world every day, major decisions are being made and careers advanced or slowed because of good - or bad - presentations.

The moral to this story? No matter what the occasion or audience, be serious about your presentations. Bring to your presentation skills the same standards of quality and excellence you apply to your product or service. Know your audience, and plan what you are going to say or visualize. Do a *"test run."* Our presentations suffer from too little or no rehearsal, not from too much. Be upbeat and enthusiastic. Put your best foot forward. You never know who may be listening to your **"MOMENT OF TRUTH."**

ZIPPER

Be sure it is zipped and that everything else is in order! This is one of the first and most embarrassing lessons learned by young boys, and grown men sometimes still forget. *(Probably another reason we build lecterns to stand behind!)*

Before you go to the front of the room, make a final check of your appearance. Buttons buttoned? Hair in place? Scarf or tie straight? Men, watch the flaps on your coat pockets. Women, watch your jewelry . . . Keep it simple, and leave the jangling bracelets at home.

Make your final check in private or discreetly. We want you to look **"put together,"** but we don't like seeing you primp or preen.

Coaching -- Individual or Groups

A Significant Opportunity About To Happen?
We Offer INDIVIDUAL or GROUP COACHING when you . . .

- Are preparing for a job interview.

- Have to meet the press.

- Need to use a teleprompter.

- Are meeting with securities analysts.

- Face an all-important presentation.

Corporate Workshops

We offer IN-HOUSE TRAINING tailored to suit your company's needs. These are ONE-HALF, ONE and TWO-DAY interactive programs that include the following topics:

Customer Service
Executive Speech Coaching
Media Training
Presentation Skills
Public Speaking
Sell Yourself, Sell Your NEW Company
Solving Communication Problems
Communicate Better In-Between Speeches and Presentations
Train The Trainer

Keynote Speeches
for your company or organization
Some popular titles are:

When The Horse You Are Riding Is Dead, Dismount!

It's Never Over!

The Best Public Speakers Study At The Zoo!

The Grass Won't Grow If You Don't!

Don't Let The Messenger They Shoot Be You!

(On your request, Mr. Jousan will taylor a speech for your group!)

Visit our web site today and order a no-frills copy of

no-frills copy $ 6.50
(either Word Perfect or Microsoft Word format)

or e.mail your request to:
information@clearcommunication.com

http://www.clearcommunication.com

Order a hard copy for a friend!

"Don't Let The Messenger They Shoot Be You!"
Book $9.95

I understand that I may return the books or tapes for a full
refund - for any reason, no questions asked.

☎ **Telephone orders:** Call Toll Free 1 (800) 544-9551

Have your Credit Card ready. we accept American Express,
Visa, Master Card, and Discover Card

✴ **Fax orders:** (480) 607-9311

✉ **Postal Orders:** Clear Communication Books,

6453 North 77th Place, Suite 7

Scottsdale, AZ 85250

NOTE: Products purchased for professional purposes
may be a tax-deductible expense.

Shipping & Handling Charges ($4.00 per book)

Sales tax (Arizona residents only)

Please use order form on page 128

Order Form

❑ _____Books   @ $9.95   _____

Shipping & Handling
_____x $4.00   _____
Sales tax (Arizona residents) 7.1%   _____

TOTAL $_____

❑ Check   ❑ Money Order payable to:

    Clear Communication Books
    6453 North 77th Place, Suite 7
    Scottsdale, AZ 85250

❑ Visa   ❑ MasterCard

❑ Discover   ❑ American Express

Credit Card number:

_____

Name on card:_____

Exp. date:___/___Signature:_____

Telephone number: (   )_____

SHIP TO: PLEASE PRINT (credit card billing address)

Name:_____

Address:_____

City:_____State:___Zip:_____